COOKED?

COOKED?

The Homosexualization
of the Entire
American Culture

Jo Coleman

Unity Press
O'Fallon, Illinois

Scriptures taken from the Holy Bible, New International Version®, NIV®. Copyright © 1973, 1978, 1984, 2011 by Biblica, Inc.™ Used by permission of Zondervan. All rights reserved worldwide. www.zondervan.com The "NIV" and "New International Version" are trademarks registered in the United States Patent and Trademark Office by Biblica, Inc.™

ISBN-10: 0-9798212-1-5
ISBN-13: 978-0-9798212-1-9

Published by Unity Press
O'Fallon, Illinois

To my husband

PREFACE

In one of C. S. Lewis' most popular books, he entitled a chapter "Sexual Morality." He said one person might say something and yet mean something different. For example, he said people might make the following statement: "Sex is nothing to be ashamed of." He said people who say that mean one of two things:

1. "There is nothing to be ashamed of in the fact that the human race reproduces itself in a certain way, nor in the fact that it gives pleasure."

2. "[T]he state into which the sexual instinct has now got is nothing to be ashamed of."

Lewis agreed with statement number one but said if people mean definition number two, "sex is nothing to be ashamed of," then they would be wrong. He said media "associates the idea of sexual indulgence with the ideas of health, normality, youth, frankness, and good humour. [And that] association is a lie." He said it is based on a truth though, because sex (without the excesses and abuses) in itself is good and is healthy. He said, "The lie consists in the suggestion that any sexual act to which you are tempted at the moment is also healthy and normal."

CONTENTS

INTRODUCTION

The premise of frogs sitting in water that is slowly heated until they die has been questioned and may not be true. However, it gives people a visual for any number of arguments. I used it on the cover to illustrate how many adults in America have no idea about the forces that are at work in their children's, and for that matter, the general public's, lives. My purpose in writing this book is to alert Americans to what is going on, and call them to get involved in standing up for what they believe.

My intent is not to deny the rights of, nor to condemn, those who have same-sex attractions. I believe those attractions are real and strong in many people's lives. However, I believe the answer is not to embrace those attractions, but instead to do one's best to overcome them.

ACKNOWLEDGMENTS

I would like to thank the following people for their contributions to this book. Thank you to my husband, who gave me up to the computer for several weeks as I finished working on this project. Thank you to my sister and daughters for their help in editing the book. Thanks to my professional editor for the final edit. And a big thank you to my niece for helping with the cover art.

Part **I**

THE BASICS

*It is only a question of using words
so that we can all understand what is
being said.*

~C. S. Lewis

DEFINITIONS

The Definition of Homosexuality

Our vocabulary allows us to communicate with others. Some words have several meanings, e.g., the word "pick" has more than twenty definitions in the dictionary. The word "homosexuality" has two meanings:

1. Sexual desire for others of one's own sex

2. Sexual activity with another of the same sex

Dictionaries define words based on their usage in the culture. If a person has same-sex desires, the dictionary (and our culture) would say they are homosexual. There is not a different word in our dictionary for one who acts on those desires.

Cooked?

That is unfortunate. The desire to do something and the doing of something are not the same, whether you are speaking about good behavior or bad behavior. The young person who desires to be a piano player, but never practices, is not a pianist. The person who is tempted to steal, yet never acts on that impulse, is not called a thief. However, a person who has same-sex desires, yet never acts on those desires, is labeled a homosexual by our culture.

Homophobia and Heterosexism

Homophobia—The word homophobia is not in most dictionaries. However, the following definition can be found at mer-riam-webster.com (m-w.com): Homophobia is an "irrational fear of, aversion to, or discrimination against homosexuality or homosexuals." A "homophobe" is a person who has such feelings or acts in this way. "Homophobic" is the adjective used to describe these people.

When people call others racists or bigots, they are not complimenting them; the words convey a very negative meaning. The word "homophobe" falls into the same category; it carries a very negative meaning.

Christians (and others) are labeled homophobic because they speak out against the normalizing of homosexual behavior in our culture. Most of them do not have an irrational fear of homosexuality or homosexuals, they simply believe that engaging in homosexual activity is immoral.

Heterosexism—M-w.com defines the word as "discrimination or prejudice by heterosexuals against homosexuals." At a conference, a gentleman once said our entire culture is heterosexist because its preferred orientation is heterosexuality. This man was correct in that our American culture has always given its approval to heterosexual unions, and until recently, frowned on homosexual ones.

Homosexuals consider not being able to be open and accepted in our culture discriminatory. They might label anyone who does not accept or affirm their lifestyle a homophobe or a heterosexist.

Other Definitions

DOMA (The Defense of Marriage Act)—When gay "marriage" was first introduced in our country, many people were worried that if one state passed it, all states would have to recognize those marriages. DOMA was passed by Congress in 1996. Section two of the law said no state would be required to recognize out-of-state gay "marriages." Section three defined marriage as between one man and one woman for federal purposes. In June of 2013, the Supreme Court of the United States (SCOTUS), overturned section three by ruling that same-sex "spouses" are eligible for federal benefits. However, it left section two intact by ruling that individual states are still allowed to decide how marriage will be defined for their citizens.

Don't Ask, Don't Tell (DADT)—This was the military's policy

that allowed gay members to serve, but to keep the fact that they were homosexual private. DADT was made law in 1993, and its repeal became effective in 2011. Since that time, gays can be open about their sexuality and still continue to serve.

ENDA (Employment Non-Discrimination Act) has been brought up for a vote during several sessions of Congress. This bill would make it unlawful for employers to discriminate in hiring based on sexual orientation. That means employers would be required to give homosexuals the same opportunities even if they were open about their chosen lifestyle. If a homosexual didn't get the job, he/she could take the company to court claiming it was discrimination.

LGBT (or GLBT)—This acronym stands for Lesbian, Gay, Bisexual, and Transgender. Sometimes you will see a Q added that could stand for Queer or Questioning. Questioning are those who have not defined themselves yet.

Marriage equality—If people want to market something that carries a negative name, they give it a different name. For example, abortion is called being pro-choice. The terms "same-sex marriage" and "gay marriage" make some people very uncomfortable, so promoters gave it a new name—marriage equality.

Prop 8—Proposition 8, also known as Prop 8, was a referendum voted on by the people of California in 2008. They voted by a fifty-two percent majority to add to their state Constitution that marriage would be between a man and a woman. A federal judge overturned that decision when it was taken to court. Proponents of Prop 8 appealed to SCOTUS. The Supreme Court ruled that the proponents didn't have the legal standing required to defend the law. Therefore, SCOTUS ruled the federal judge's decision would stand. Gay "marriage" in California was thus legalized by the courts.

Sexual orientation—When you have and/or act on same-sex attractions exclusively, you are considered homosexual. When you are attracted to and/or engage in sex with both sexes, you are considered bisexual. If you are attracted to and/or engage in sex with only the opposite sex, you are considered heterosexual.

Transgender or Transsexual—These are people who are physically one sex, but feel internally that they are the other. Some transgendered people dress and act like the opposite sex. Others have surgical procedures and hormone therapy to change their sex. (When the words "gender identity" or "gender expression" appear in print, they refer to transgendered people.)

Part **II**

IS IT ANY WONDER?

Why People under 35 Largely Support Gay "Marriage"

Education

1

ELEMENTARY ED.
(K-4th Grade)

GLSEN: Gay, Lesbian & Straight Education Network

Have your children or grandchildren participated in a public school program called "No Name-Calling Week?" Schools have been conducting this program since 2004. Reading through the curriculum and suggested reading list, it appears to be a good way to teach children that name-calling and bullying are hurtful and wrong. If presenters of the course are offended that it introduces bullying of homosexuals or bullying of children being raised in homosexual homes, they could simply preview the materials and take those parts out. However, that is not what the creators of this program had in mind. GLSEN (pronounced *Glisten*) is the organization that created these materials.

GLSEN stands for the Gay, Lesbian & Straight Education Network. On the organization's website, you can find this description: "[We are] the leading national education organization focused on ensuring safe schools for all lesbian, gay, bisexual and transgender (LGBT) students."[1] (Most of the time GLSEN says "for all students.") Established in 1990 and nationally in 1995, GLSEN seeks to get all children to accept homosexuality, bisexuality and transsexuality as alternative lifestyles, without making any judgments about people who engage in these types of behavior. They target schools K-12 in our nation, but also do some of their projects on college campuses.

To get an idea of what GLSEN is involved in, here are some of their initiatives:

1. (2001) National Day of Silence[2] (one day in April): Students can wear T-shirts and remain silent (outside of classroom instruction) for the entire school day to show support of anti-bullying and no name-calling of LGBT people.

2. (2004) No Name-Calling Week (one week in January): Any adult (usually counselors or teachers) in a school setting can order materials for an

"annual week of educational activities aimed at ending name-calling"[3] and for beginning an "on-going dialogue about ways to eliminate bullying."[4]

3. (2005) Ally Week (a week in October) "is a week for students to identify, support and celebrate Allies against anti-LGBT . . . language, bullying and harassment in America's schools."[5]

4. (2011) Changing the Game: This program seeks to make sports in our nation's schools LGBT inclusive.[6]

GLSEN recommends several ways schools can be inclusive. A few are:

- [A]llow . . . transgender students to . . . use locker rooms according to their gender identity.

- Dress codes/uniforms for physical education students are gender-neutral.

- All communications to and programs for parents/ caregivers of athletes use language that is inclusive of diverse families, including those headed by same-sex partners.[7]

All of GLSEN's programs target impressionable young people. The organization is promoting these materials not just in public schools, but in private schools as well.

Bullying Policies

Stopbullying.gov, a federal government website managed by the U.S. Department of Health and Human Services, claims that all fifty states have laws and/or policies that forbid bullying in schools.

Many states are seeking to make their anti-bullying policies stricter. Minnesota is one such state. Presently its policy is a simple thirty-seven words:

> Each school board shall adopt a written policy prohibiting intimidation and bullying of any student. The policy shall address intimidation and bullying in all forms, including, but not limited to, electronic forms and forms involving Internet use.[8]

Six students who were bullied "for real or perceived sexual orientation"[9] sued the Anoka-Hennepin school district. There was a federal investigation, and the lawsuit was settled by the district. In response to that incident, the governor set up a task force on the prevention of school bullying. A twenty-one-page bill entitled "The Safe and Supportive

Minnesota Schools Bill" was drafted and is now ready to be voted on.

Katherine Kersten, who works for a conservative organization, Center for the American Experiment, testified before the assembly. She said:

> [A]nti-bullying legislation isn't driven by a dramatic increase in bullying. Instead, it's trying to push a political and social agenda some families don't agree with, particularly homosexuality and gay marriage.
>
> [T]he bill also allows anyone to claim they are a victim of bullying and would protect certain classes of students more than others, particularly on sexual orientation.
>
> It would send the message to students in protected groups that they have an absolute right not to have their feelings hurt or their views challenged.[10]

2

MIDDLE AND
HIGH SCHOOLS

Gay-Straight Alliances

Under the list of clubs at your local high school, you might find a club entitled GSA. GSA stands for Gay-Straight Alliance. Because they want to steer clear of the stigma attached to a club name beginning with the word "Gay," some clubs go by alternative names, e.g., "Project Rainbow," "Pride Alliance," "Common Ground," "Coexist", "Spectrum," or even the "Straight-Gay Alliance."

The first GSA was started about 1988 by a gentleman who had experienced "taunting and bullying" in his school years because of his perceived effeminate behavior. Young people should not have to endure abuse because of their effeminate (in boys) and masculine (in girls) behavior. However, is establishing clubs where young people affirm one another's self-identifying as gay the correct way to address the problem?

The GSA Network strives to support GSAs across the country. There are currently 4000[1] registered GSAs nationwide. As of May 2013, there were over 900[2] GSAs established in middle schools or junior highs in just the state of California.

In June 2012, Ontario, Canada passed a law called the Accepting Schools Act. Consider the reach of this anti-bullying legislation:

> The bill states that no school board or principal shall be able to deny students the right to establish student lead groups. That means, even in private schools, students have the right to start gay-straight alliances, and if the administration objects they can be taken to court.[3]

Greenhaven Press: Indoctrination at Its Finest

If your high school student is asked to do a paper on any given social topic, from poverty to prisons, they might run across a series of books called "Opposing Viewpoints" published by

Cooked?

Greenhaven Press.

"Greenhaven Press continues to set the standard as a leading producer of quality nonfiction for the high school library market,"[4] is the claim made on the publisher's website. The publisher is targeting high school students, and many of the books can be found in young adult libraries.

The Opposing Viewpoints series goes back as far as 1971. Our local library system carries almost a thousand of their books, and more than one hundred of these books have publication dates later than 2011.

Here's the premise for the books: Essays on several topics are chosen to represent the arguments for both the liberal and conservative view of any given topic. It appears that each side gets equal time. However, in reading the introductions to the books, one gets the idea that the books were compiled and edited by liberal-minded people.

One example of this liberal bias is the book *Homosexuality* by Noah Berlatsky. Mr. Berlatsky quotes several gay websites to back up his proposition that homosexuality has been around a while and in various cultures. The book leans heavily toward acceptance of homosexuality.

Mr. Berlatsky included in the book a conservative article on the Catholic stance toward homosexuality. However, in the book's Table of Contents, he writes, "[The] Catholic Church has no prejudice against those who commit homosexual acts." This is a true statement, but misleading. The Catholic Church is not prejudiced against active homosexuals, but it does hold strong convictions that homosexual acts are wrong.

FLAG and FOX with a P

Parents and Friends of Lesbian and Gays (PFLAG) was founded in 1972. The organization teaches parents to love their gay children and embrace the lifestyle those children have chosen. On its website, PFLAG says it is "committed to advancing equality through its mission of support, education and advocacy."[5] It boasts 350 chapters and 200,000 supporters, with a presence in all fifty states.[6]

I attended a PFLAG meeting. A good part of the meeting was geared toward advocacy. There was a bill being considered in the legislature, and the group was organizing a bus trip to take people to the state capitol to lobby legislators. Someone in the group was working on contacting the local school counselors to make sure they were aware of PFLAG. He would then give them PFLAG's contact information so that young people who were dealing with same-sex attractions might be referred to their group.

Gay activists claim people are born gay, and that they can never change. However, some people who once identified as gay, leave that lifestyle and either remain chaste or lead a heterosexual lifestyle. These ex-gays are targeted by gay activists who claim they were either never gay in the first place, or that they are being untrue to their identity, that of being homosexual. Ex-gays who for many years were mocked or ridiculed for being gay, find that they are now ridiculed by the very community that they were once a part of. Ex-gays might be the most persecuted people group in America today.

Cooked?

Parents and Friends of Ex-Gays and Gays (PFOX) was founded in 1998. The organization supports ex-gays in their decision to leave their former lifestyle. PFOX also acts as a support group for parents whose children are gay. The group encourages parents to unconditionally love their children. However, the group does not encourage parents to affirm their child's lifestyle.

PFOX encourages young people to postpone self-identifying as gay until adulthood, because sexual attractions are something that can and do change over time. A 2005 study claims that a group of same-sex attracted boys were tested one year later and only eleven percent still identified as being exclusively same-sex attracted.[7]

PFOX says this is what is happening in the schools:

> Unlike gay groups, ex-gay groups like PFOX are routinely denied equal access to participate in public school events, donate books to public school libraries, and present speakers on diversity day.[8]

Some schools are encouraging children to self-identify as gay, and at the same time trying to keep them from hearing alternate views.

3

COLLEGES AND
UNIVERSITIES

Even in Christian Colleges

Many of our college and university campuses have groups that support LGBT individuals. At Harvard there is the "Harvard Gay & Lesbian Caucus." Yale has three support groups:

- Lesbian, Gay, Bisexual Graduate Students—Outland
- Lesbian, Gay, Bisexual Law Students' Association (LGBLSA)

Cooked?

- Lesbian, Gay, Bisexual, and Transgender Cooperative at Yale[1]

Arizona State University lists ten LGBT groups.[2]

This is not only happening on secular college campuses. Southern Methodist University in Dallas Texas has had an LGBT student group called Spectrum since 1991. At Gustavus Adolphus College (Lutheran) in St. Peter, MN, one group is called Queers and Allies, or Q&A. The 2010 freshman orientation at this college included a skit.[3] Laurie Higgins, who works for the Illinois Family Institute, described it this way:

> [The skit] begins with this whimsical rhyme: "Follow along and listen quite clear to learn of the wonderful world of the queer." It again features ignorant, irresponsible upperclassmen, this time defining the terms lesbian, gay, pansexual, bi-curious, bisexual, transgender and transsexual for freshmen, explaining, for example, that lesbian women "make love quite beautifully," and that the term "bi-curious" refers to "testin' the waters, seein' what's attractive." . . .
>
> Next a boy waxes romantic about his male lover and a girl proclaims, "I happen to be a lesbian — a big one. And my, oh my, I love it. All the women, the flowy hair, the sweet perfume, mmm, mmm. I like sex. I *love* sex."[4]

Some Christian colleges would like to keep a traditional biblical view of homosexuality. However, they are taking
some heat for doing so.

Soulforce is an organization seeking to free LGBTQ people from "religious and political oppression."[5] It sponsors the
Equality Ride, a bus tour with several young gay activists. Every year they travel to colleges, especially Christian colleges.
They give the colleges advance notice that they are coming.
If they are welcomed, they try to get a public hearing where
they can share their viewpoints and materials with students
and staff. If they are not welcomed, they protest in order to
gain media attention.

Silencing Dissent

Most of us are familiar with neon yellow signs that say "School
Zone" or give a reduced speed limit if children are present.
The sign might even say "School Safety Zone."

But have you ever seen a sign that simply says "Safe
Zone?" The Safe Zone Program is a project of the Gay Alliance. "[It] was created to develop, enhance and maintain environments in workplaces, schools and other social settings
that are culturally competent and supportive to LGBT individuals, as well as straight identified people who care about
diversity, equality and inclusion."[6]

The program trains people how to be supportive of LGBT
people. After the training sessions, people are allowed to use
a decal with the words "Safe Zone" on it. The Gay Alliance

says a safe zone might be "a room, a car, or an entire college campus."

LGBT groups in colleges are enjoying this opportunity. It seems each group can design its own decal. Some of the decals use common LGBT symbols or colors. The six colors of the rainbow flag are often used. You'll sometimes see an inverted triangle or the transgender symbol, which is a combination of the female and the male symbol. The transgender symbol might also have added to it the combined male-female sign on the top left (see below). However, the distinguishing characteristic of the safe zone decals is that most include the words "safe zone."

| Female | Male | Transgender |

Colleges are conducting training sessions for those who would like to establish a safe zone on their campus. The Center for Social Justice hosts monthly Safe Zone Training sessions at the University of Nevada, Las Vegas.[7] At Rhodes College in Tennessee, more than 140 students have been through the program, and their Counseling Center offers five to seven sessions each year.[8]

With many students (and faculty) openly supporting the gay lifestyle, might students with an alternate view just choose to keep their opinions to themselves?

Part **III**

IS IT ANY WONDER?

**Why People under 35
Largely Support Gay
"Marriage"**

Other Influences

4

THE INTERNET

Answering the "Am I Gay?" Question

If a young person types, "Am I gay?" into an internet search engine, they can find a variety of answers. Consider the following:

- From a highly respected university's website:

  > The only person who can answer your question, "Am I gay," is you.
  >
  > Sometimes, the only way to find out what really turns you on is to reach for the light switch and explore your feelings in search of inner peace.[1]

Cooked?

- From a general information site:

> The best way to determine if you are gay is to explore your sexuality. Experiment with your attractions.
>
> Are you attracted . . . on a sexual and emotional level . . . ?[2]

- From a personal website:

> If, as you get older, you start having more consistent fantasies or desires regarding your same-gender classmates, then yes, there is a very good chance that you are gay.
>
> Search your soul. Carefully consider your sexual fantasies and desires. You will eventually come to know.[3]

All of these sites tell people to search within themselves to find out what will make them happy.

The internet is a place that young people searching for answers are encouraged to experiment with different sexual activity and then choose the one that "really turns them on."

It Gets Better

The "It Gets Better" Campaign was started in September 2010 by gay activist Dan Savage. His intent was to slow the teen suicide rate among gays. He thought he could accomplish this by encouraging gay teens to take pride in their identity as homosexuals. He told them that if they just persevere, things will get better as they grow up. Mr. Savage posted a video on You Tube and invited others to post similar videos. Today the organization claims that people have uploaded 50,000[4] videos where they encourage gay teens to hang on to the hope that it does get better.

It's one thing to be encouraged to continue pursuing the gay lifestyle locally, but you can go online and hear a vast multitude telling you that you are OK just like you are. President Obama and Hillary Clinton have joined this multitude.

In regard to teen suicide, an article in the Official Journal of the American Academy of Pediatrics made this claim: "For each year's delay in bisexual or homosexual self-labeling, the odds of a suicide attempt diminish by eighty percent."[5]

5

TELEVISION

Prime Time

In 2009, the Neilsen Co. tracked TV viewing habits of age groups two through five and five through eight, and the Kaiser Family Foundation tracked the same for eight to eighteen year-olds. Both companies found that their tracked viewers (two to eighteen year-olds) watched an average of about four to four and a half hours of television a day.[1] If these young viewers watch prime time TV (7–10 p.m. or 8–11 p.m., depending on the time zone), will they see any LGBT characters?

In 1977, ABC was about to air its premiere of the sitcom Soap. It was the first time a gay character was featured on America's prime time TV. Several church denominations raised opposition to the show because of various moral concerns, but the outcries came up empty. The show aired and continued for four seasons.

From 1977 to present day, we notice a dramatic change in the number of actors/actresses that portray gay, lesbian, bisexual and transgender (LGBT) characters. Seventeen years ago, GLAAD (Gay and Lesbian Alliance Against Defamation) began filing a report called "Where are we on TV?" The organization calculates the percentage of LGBT characters.

In 2007, on prime time TV, GLAAD claimed the percentage was at 1.1.[2] In 2012, that number moved up to 4.4 percent.[3] The Neilsen website puts this quote in a news story: "Teen and Millennial viewers . . . dedicated over a third of their prime time scripted TV viewing to series depicting at least one regular or recurring LGBT character."[4]

TV programming has made homosexuality "normal." One article stated that the programming seems to be targeted at teens. An Entertainment Weekly columnist writes, "[Y]outh-oriented networks lead the way with LGBT representation; ABC Family and MTV rank at the top of GLAAD's annual Network Responsibility index, and TeenNick's *Degrassi* has included a staggering eight non-straight characters (including this season's female-to-male transgender teen, Adam)."[5] This same columnist said the last frontier is the preteens, as only Disney and Nickelodeon have yet to show gay characters.

Cooked?

Ellen DeGeneres

Ellen DeGeneres has become a household name in America. She got her start in stand-up comedy and moved to acting during the late '80s and '90s. In 1997, she made public that she is a lesbian. Since 2003, she has been hosting The Ellen DeGeneres show. It is one of the most-watched day-time talk shows.

Ellen has probably done more to advance the cause of gay rights than any other person. Because she is very talented as a TV personality, and appears to America to be "normal," many people have concluded that gay people should be accepted for who they are. They have decided that gays should be able to marry and adopt children just like heterosexuals.

6

WHAT ELSE?

How Pop Music Affects Our Children

Our young people are affected by popular music in three ways: by the lyrics of songs, by the effect popular singers have on their admirers, and by the money wealthy artists give to advocacy groups.

Consider the lyrics of songs, like the 2008 song entitled "I Kissed a Girl" from a popular female artist. It includes these lines:

> I kissed a girl and I liked it
> It felt so wrong
> It felt so right
>
> It's not what,

Cooked?

> Good girls do
> Not how they should behave
> My head gets so confused
> Hard to obey
>
> Ain't no big deal, it's innocent[1]

Same Love, a song by the artist Macklemore (July, 2012), includes the following lines:

> When I was in the 3rd grade
> I thought that I was gay
> Cause I could draw, my uncle was
> And I kept my room straight

In the chorus of the song a lesbian sings:

> And I can't change
> Even if I tried
> Even if I wanted to[2]

Not many songs have these strictly homosexual themes, but there are some.

A second effect of popular music is that some young people idolize famous artists and follow their every move; they want to be just like the singers they adore.

There are a number of female artists who publicly support gay rights. If a young person's favorite artist is supporting a cause, then the young person may desire to be supportive as well. One young female artist who supports gay rights says, "I never could have imagined how much impact my music could have on people. I realized that through pop music, I have the opportunity to stand up for something I believe in."[3]

The final effect of popular music is monetary. Top tier musicians earn a lot of money. If they support organizations with just a small amount of their earnings, they can dramatically increase the influences of these organizations.

You Know Someone

Do you remember during your growing-up years (6-18) meeting anyone who fit the gay stereotype? A young male might have been more comfortable spending time with the girls, and he was very "nice." He might have displayed some feminine mannerisms or speech, or he might have been over-the-top flamboyant.

Let's call this young man Jerrod. It seems to Jerrod's friends that he was born that way, and even if he wanted to, he couldn't change his personality. When Jerrod tells his friends he is gay, no one is surprised. Jerrod's friends think that he should not be condemned to a life of loneliness simply because he can't find that woman who will fulfill him as a partner. The friends conclude that Jerrod should be allowed to date and marry someone who will accept him as he is. Isn't that the compassionate thing to do? Jerrod's friends support gay marriage because of Jerrod.

Cooked?

This is the story of countless young Americans. They may not have been indoctrinated in our schools, but because they know someone who is gay, they choose to support gay rights.

Part **IV**

THE CULTURE IS SHIFTING

If you are on the wrong road,
progress means doing an about-turn
and walking back to the right road.

~C. S. Lewis

7

THE CHURCH

Division in the Ranks

Organized religion is the biggest obstacle to affirming the gay lifestyle. If gay activists can show that religions are divided on this issue, it will allow them to do away with the final roadblock that is keeping them from being part of the mainstream.

Religious groups that are steadfast in their condemnation of homosexual behavior are Catholics, evangelical Protestants, Orthodox Jews, Muslims, and Mormons.

Several offshoots of the above religions formed when members who were reluctant to abandon their faith, yet didn't want to give up their lifestyle, started "gay-friendly" organizations within their churches. Almost every religion has these groups. Many of them started after 1970.

Major denominations allow homosexuality, e.g., the Episcopal Church, Unitarian Universalists and the United Church of Christ. However, in these churches, many members (and perhaps even some entire congregations), hold to the biblical view that homosexual acts are sinful.

Metropolitan Community Churches, which include 23,000[1] members worldwide, are attended mostly by gay churchgoers.

When the culture sees religious organizations divided on the issue of homosexuality, it gives activists great hope.

What is Happening in Our Seminaries?

In 2001, an organization called the Religious Institute was formed. On its website, the Religious Institute uses the phrase "sexual health." One gets the impression that "sexual health" means "gay rights." This goal of LGBT inclusion is listed in the organization's "Religious Declaration on Sexual Morality, Justice, and Healing." In this document, the Religious Institute states that it seeks:

> Full inclusion of . . . LGBT persons in congregational life, including their ordination and marriage equality.[2]

In 2008, the Religious Institute started a project intended "to improve the curricula, policies and institutional environments of the nation's seminaries." In other words, the organization wanted to make seminaries LGBT inclusive.

Since 2008, the Religious Institute has gotten three leading seminaries to sign on as pilot sites; these pilot sites committed themselves to making "significant, campus-wide changes." The three seminaries to try out the LGBT inclusive initiatives were Brite Divinity School (Christian Church [Disciples of Christ]) in Fort Worth, Texas, the Jewish Theological Seminary in New York City, and Yale's Divinity School in New Haven, Connecticut.

The Unitarian Universalist Association became the first major denomination in the country to require that candidates for ordination be educated with materials produced or recommended by the Religious Institute. The Religious Institute is making inroads into several other denominations as well, such as Episcopal, United Methodist, Presbyterian Church of USA, and American Baptist. The organization claims that twenty-seven seminaries now meet its criteria for a "sexually healthy and responsible seminary," whereas only ten met its criteria in 2009.[3] The Religious Institute is currently encouraging the Association of Theological Schools, the accrediting body for U.S. seminaries, to adopt its ideas and make "sexual health" required courses for seminarians.

8

GOVERNMENT

It's the Law

To see how far our nation has moved in favor of the gay lifestyle, one needs only to look at gay-friendly laws (to include rights for transgender individuals) in many states and on the national level.

Gay-friendly Laws:

1. Non-discrimination laws are those that include the words "sexual orientation" (homosexuals) and "gender identity/expression" (transsexuals). If you are a landlord or an employer, you may not deny housing or employment to people because

they are homosexual or transgendered. The Employment Non-Discrimination Act is generally referred to as ENDA.

In schools, students or teachers who are morally opposed to homosexuality or transsexuality may not state their opinion lest they offend (discriminate against) people of that persuasion. This legislation is called the Student Non-Discrimination Act (SNDA).

2. Domestic Partnerships, Civil Unions, and Gay "Marriage:" Domestic partnerships give some benefits to same sex couples. Civil unions give many more benefits. (Some people say civil unions give gay "couples" most of the benefits that married people have; it's just not called marriage.) Same-sex "marriage" makes a gay couples' union equal to any wedded couple.

In the thirteen states where gay "marriage" is legal, it has been decided in the following ways:

- The courts imposed gay "marriage" on four states (MA, IA, CT, and CA).

- State legislatures passed the laws in six states (NY, VT, NH, RI, DE, and MN).

- In 2012, the people voted (ME, MD, and

> WA). (Activists won the people over by always framing the issue as one of equality. One source says traditionalists were outspent three-to-one.[1])

3. Adoption Laws: In all fifty states, single gay people can adopt. Some states limit adoptions by gay "couples."

4. Hate Crime Laws: If you commit a crime against a homosexual or transsexual and it is determined you have a bias against them because they are that way, you can be sentenced to much harsher penalties.

5. No anti-gay counseling for minors (even if that's what the minor wants): In September 2012, California passed this type of law. The following are excerpts from it:

> Under no circumstances shall a mental health provider engage in sexual orientation change efforts (SOCE) with a patient under 18 years of age . . . Any sexual orientation change efforts attempted on a patient under 18 years of age by a mental health provider shall be considered unprofessional conduct and shall subject a

mental health provider to discipline by the licensing entity for that mental health provider.[2]

A bill pending in the New Jersey senate says no licensed professional counselor can engage in this type of counseling.[3]

Number of states that have passed gay-friendly legislation:

Type of Law	# States
1. **Non-discrimination laws:**	
In housing	21 [4]
In employment	21 [5]
In schools (anti-bullying laws/policies)	50 [6]
2. **Benefits for same-sex "couples:"**	
Only domestic partnerships	3 [7]
Civil unions added	4 [8]
Same-sex "marriage"	13 (+DC)[9]
3. **Adoptions by gay "couples"**	19 (+DC)[10]
4. **Hate crime legislation**	
Sexual orientation	31 (+DC)[11]
Gender identity	13 (+DC)[12]
5. **No anti-gay counseling for minors**	1

Gay-friendly legislation at the national level:

Type of Law	National Legislation
1. **Non-discrimination laws:**	
In federal housing	Passed 2012
In employment (ENDA)	Considered during the 2011-2012 session
In schools (SNDA)	Considered during the 2011-2012 session
2. **Benefits for same-sex "couples:"**	Major provision of DOMA repealed by Supreme Court in June 2013
3. **Hate crime legislation**	Matthew Shepard Act Passed 2009
4. **Gays can serve in military**	Closeted (1993)—DADT Openly (2011)—DADT Repealed

Many of our large cities have drafted ordinances that give homosexuals the rights mentioned above.

A Democrat Issue

Until recent years, most members in both of our major political parties, Democrats and Republicans, stated publicly that they were for natural marriage, as opposed to same-sex "marriage." The first major break from that trend came in 2012, when President Obama said he had evolved on the issue and now supports same-sex "marriage."

Every presidential election year, a group of leaders in each party draft the core beliefs of the party. The 2012 National Democratic Platform on this issue reads:

Freedom to Marry

We support the right of all families to have equal respect, responsibilities, and protections under the law. We support marriage equality and support the movement to secure equal treatment under law for same-sex couples. . . .

We oppose discriminatory federal and state constitutional amendments and other attempts to deny equal protection of the laws to committed same-sex couples who seek the same respect and responsibilities as other married couples. We support the full repeal of the so-called Defense of Marriage Act . . .[13]

Cooked?

The 2012 National Republican Platform reads:

Preserving and Protecting Traditional Marriage

The institution of marriage is the foundation of civil society. . . . It has been proven by both experience and endless social science studies that traditional marriage is best for children. . . . The success of marriage directly impacts the economic well-being of individuals. Furthermore, the future of marriage affects freedom. The lack of family formation not only leads to more government costs, but also to more government control over the lives of its citizens in all aspects. . . . [W]e believe that marriage, the union of one man and one woman must be upheld as the national standard, a goal to stand for, encourage, and promote through laws governing marriage. . . .[14]

Some might say national politics do not affect politics at the local level. However, a recent vote in the state of Illinois shows how local politics reflect national politics. When the Illinois Senate voted to approve gay "marriage" eighty-two percent of the Democrats, but only one Republican, voted for it.

Another example of how gay "marriage" has become primarily a Democrat issue is the vote for it in the New York

Assembly. Ninety-six percent of Democrats and less than thirteen percent of Republicans voted for it.

Tim Gill-The Strategist

Tim Gill,[15] a native of Colorado, started Quark Inc., which later became the very successful computer software company QuarkXPress. In 1994, he started the Gill Foundation, which seeks to advance equality for LGBT people and people with HIV/AIDS. To date, the Gill Foundation has donated $220 million to this work.[16]

In 2000, Mr. Gill left QuarkXPress and became involved in political activism. His strategy was to focus on state races and initiatives rather than work at the national level. Since national Senate races usually cost more than $10 million and national House races cost more than $1.5 million,[17] he determined he could spend his money more effectively by putting that money into state races. A winning state Senate campaign rarely reaches the million dollar mark and sometimes costs less than $10,000.[18]

In Colorado (2004), with the help of four other wealthy donors, Gill's political machine outspent Republicans and won enough races to change both houses of the state legislature from Republican to Democrat. In 2008, Democrats made further gains in the legislature and a Democratic governor was elected.

Gill is not just focused on Colorado. He was able to solicit enough donations for an Iowa legislator's opponent to unseat him. Danny Carroll did not realize he had been the target of gay activism until he was out of office. His offense was that he had sponsored a bill in Iowa that would have banned gay "marriage."

The political activity of Gill might be compared to those generals who wage war. Gill has all the states mapped out as far as state legislature makeup (Democrat and Republican). He also keeps abreast of all the bills that are being considered. He then determines where his money will best be spent. He sends this information out to those who are willing to give to the cause. And—voilà—he's winning battles all across America.

9

NATIONAL
ORGANIZATIONS

The American Psychiatric Association

In 1973, the American Psychiatric Association decided to remove homosexuality from its list of mental disorders.[1] This was accomplished through pressure from the gay rights lobby. It's a little complicated, but the facts are:

1. For four years (since 1968), gay rights activists worked hard to get homosexuality removed from that list.

2. A panel consisting of people from three pro-gay

groups wrote a letter to APA members (never stating that it came from a biased group) asking for a volunteer response.

3. Only one-third of the eligible psychiatrists responded.[2] Those who did respond voted sixty/forty in favor of removing homosexuality from the mental disorders list. (That would mean only about twenty percent of the eligible psychiatrists voted to remove it.)

4. The next year it was removed, despite grave concerns of some of the members.

5. In 1977, (without pressure from a gay-rights lobby) a survey went out to 2,500 psychiatrists asking whether homosexuality was a disorder: sixty-nine percent responded yes, eighteen percent no, and thirteen percent were undecided.[3]

Even today, there is hardly a consensus among the scientific community that homosexuality is normal.

Political Activists

After the American Psychiatric Association changed its policy about homosexuality not being a disorder (1973), the American Psychological Association (also known as the APA) quickly followed suit (1975). The National Education Association (NEA) and a whole host of other organizations then jumped on the train. At first they might not have been so bold about their support for gay rights, but now they are very vocal.

The American Psychological Association is made up of fifty-four divisions. Each division has its own officers, publications, etc. Some are subgroups of psychology and others focus on topical areas, e.g., Division nineteen is the Society for Military Psychology (founded in 1938), and Division forty-four is the Society for the Psychological Study of Lesbian and Gay Issues (founded in 1985). It seems that any of these divisions individually or by working together can form task groups and do studies which, when completed, carry the full weight of the APA. Using gay activist Aaron Belkin's books for source material, in its 2004 policy statement, "Sexual Orientation and Military Service," the APA said:

- Don't Ask, Don't Tell[4] [DADT] . . . discriminates on the basis of sexual orientation, and has caused many qualified personnel to be involuntarily separated from military service solely because of their sexual orientation.[5]

- [The] APA reaffirms its strong commitment to removing the stigma of mental illness that has long been associated with homosexual and bisexual behavior and orientations.[6]

In 2005, the APA went a step further. Divisions nineteen and forty-four coordinated and decided to do a three-year study from 2005 to 2007; they wanted to know how they could implement their 2004 policy statement. They collaborated with the Service Members' Legal Defense Network, the ACLU, and the National Gay and Lesbian Task Force. Their primary goal was to do away with DADT either by law (Congress) or in the courts. They aided in congressional repeal of the law in late 2010.

The National Education Association (NEA) was not to be outdone. In early 2013, it filed amicus briefs "arguing that both Proposition 8 and DOMA should be struck down by the U.S. Supreme Court."[7] NEA president, Dennis Van Roekel, issued a statement on behalf of the NEA's more than three million members that begins, "Prop 8 and DOMA aren't just unconstitutional, they contradict American values of fairness, inclusion and freedom for all."[8]

Other professional organizations are also supporting gay rights. A 2013 technical report from the American Association of Pediatrics states that it supports marriage equality, i.e., gay "marriage."[9] The American Medical Association (AMA) posts its "Policies on GLBT Issues" on its website. Some excerpts follow:

> "Our [AMA]: . . . recognizes that denying civil
> marriage based on sexual orientation is dis-
> criminatory . . . will support legislative and
> other efforts to allow the adoption of a child by

the same-sex partner . . . asks youth oriented organizations [e.g., the Boy Scouts] to reconsider exclusionary policies that are based on sexual orientation or gender identity.[10]

The AMA also advocated for the repeal of the military's "Don't Ask, Don't Tell policy." The National Association of Social Workers (NASW) is urging Congress to pass ENDA.[11] In their June 2010 newsletter, an article is entitled "NASW Observes LGBT Pride, Touts Advocacy Efforts: Association . . . Supports Same-Sex Couples' Rights."[12]

Many of our nation's professional counseling, education, social work, and medical associations are not only LGBT-affirming, they have become political activists in this area.

Corporate America

Since 2004, conservative organizations have been calling for boycotts of various companies who have been publicly coming out in support of gay rights. Among these companies are P & G, PepsiCo, Home Depot, Walgreens, Ford, and GAP.

Why is corporate America flocking to support gay rights? These are some possibilities:

- Gay activists within the corporations seek to make their workplaces more LGBT inclusive.

- Corporations want to be on the cutting edge of

"civil rights." Many are headquartered in American cities, and cities are more accepting of homosexuality than rural America.

- The LGBT community has $790 billion of buying power, and companies want those dollars.

Or it could be due to pressure from an organization called The Human Rights Campaign (HRC). HRC, according to its website, is "the largest civil rights organization working to achieve equality for lesbian, gay, bisexual and transgender Americans."[13] Every year, HRC sends out to an increasing number of businesses (in 2012, 1,848 companies) a Corporate Equality Index survey.[14] Companies are rated by HRC on the following criteria, with the number of points awarded in parentheses:

1. Does my company include LGBT people in their equal employment opportunity policies?

   - By adding the words "sexual orientation" (homosexuals) (15)

   - By adding the words "gender identity" or "gender expression" (transgender individuals) (15)

2. Does my company offer benefits to LGBT people?

- Partner health/medical benefits (15)

- Other benefits for partners (the same as given to spouses of opposite-sex married employees), e.g., retirement annuities, travel, bereavement leave (10)

- Transgender-inclusive health insurance which pays for surgery, hormone therapy, counseling, etc. (dollar maximum on this must meet or exceed $75,000) [15] (10)

3. Does my company have diversity training that discusses LGBT issues?

    - For employees or management (10)

    - Does it have employee discussion groups (ERG's) focusing on LGBT issues, or a firm-wide Diversity Council. (10)

4. Does my company support the external LGBT community? (15)
   It must do three of the following:

    - Actively recruit LGBT employees

    - Use LGBT-owned businesses as suppliers

- Market specifically to LGBT consumers

- Support one LGBT organization or event, e.g., march in a gay pride parade

- Support LGBT causes through legislation or initiatives

If a company has "a connection with an anti-LGBT organization or activity," i.e., if it supports natural marriage, it gets 25 points subtracted from their Corporate Equality Index. In HRC's 2013 CEI, only one company, Exxon Mobil, supported natural marriage and received the dreaded 25-point demerit.

HRC claims that in 2012, 252 companies earned a perfect score of 100. Some of these corporate HQ are in very conservative states where gays have few, if any, legal privileges. However, these corporations are going out of their way to grant the entire spectrum of rights asked for by HRC. They are doing this in spite of the calls for boycotts.

Note: HRC sent out its equality surveys to American Lawyer magazine's top 200 revenue-grossing law firms, and 141 law firms participated. Law firms stand to make a bundle in taking up the cause of gay rights.

BSA: The Last Man Standing Falls

Our professional associations and corporate America openly advocate for gay rights. What was the only organization that seemed to be holding its ground against the acceptance of homosexuality? It was the Boy Scouts of America (BSA).

Boys with same-sex attractions have always been allowed in the Boy Scouts and could earn highest honors. They just were not allowed to act out openly and inappropriately. In July 2012, after an eleven-member BSA committee conducted a two-year study, it concluded its policy of excluding open and avowed homosexuals in its ranks was in the best interest of its organization.[16] How did it happen that less than one year later BSA adopted the policy to allow openly gay scouts?

Gay activists gave the scout board members a petition signed by 1.8 million people (the opposition only got 250,000 signatures)[17] asking that they change their policy to allow openly gay scouts and leaders. But that might not be what caused the change in policy. It could have been pressure from corporate donors[18] who are often pressured by The Human Rights Campaign.

Corporate donors (many who scored over 90 on HRC's Corporate Equality Index), beginning in the fall of 2012, threatened to stop their donations if the policy wasn't changed.[19] So the Boy Scouts were faced with losing a ton of money if they kept their policy in place. According to their annual financial statement, contributions to the BSA from 2011 to 2012 had already fallen over fifty percent.[20] So it seems the board members may have made the decision based on finances.

Even before their May 23rd, 2013 meeting, the Boy Scouts of America board members proposed a truce. They said they would consider allowing gay scouts, but not scout leaders. The 1,400 delegates of the BSA's National Council voted sixty percent in favor of allowing openly gay scouts.[21]

The Boy Scout Oath reads, "On my honor . . . I will do my best . . . to keep myself . . . morally straight." A majority of religious persons in America consider homosexual acts to be immoral. How will these leaders accommodate scouts who profess to be actively engaging in homosexual behavior?

The Scout Oath also says, "On my honor, I will do my best to do my duty to God." This duty to God is explained as follows:

> Your family and religious leaders teach you about God and the ways you can serve. You do your duty to God by following the wisdom of those teachings every day and by respecting and defending the rights of others to practice their own beliefs.

The new decision to allow openly gay scouts will take effect in January of 2014. Some parents are already working to establish an alternate organization that will hold to the former, stricter, moral standards.

10

THE MEDIA

Newspapers

One careful reader of a McClatchy owned newspaper made these observations over a ten-month period. This was during the time gay marriage was being considered in the state legislature.

In the letters to the editor section, writers two-to-one (22-11) were against gay marriage. In the sound off section, where writers are allowed to remain anonymous, they were against gay marriage seven to one (7-1). The paper's editorial board never published its own view, but it did use three pro-gay guest columns from a sister newspaper. In the news sections of the paper, there were almost ten-to-one (67-7) articles about gays making gains, (legislative gains, getting noteworthy endorsements, etc.) vs. natural marriage proponents holding their ground (Vatican, Boy Scouts, etc.). To be fair to the paper, gays have been making great gains here in the states and around the world; the newspaper is just reporting.

As a conservative, this reader rated news articles that appeared to promote gay rights, either by photos, headlines, or content, vs. those with the opposing view. There were about five-to-one (25-6) articles that leaned in favor of gay rights.

Large articles seeking to normalize homosexuality were printed when the legislature was debating the subject. Yet there were no reviews of books that presented the opposing viewpoint, nor were there any articles defending natural marriage.

Overall, the newspaper articles favored gay marriage more than eighty-five percent of the time.

The reader likened it to being confined to the hen house. Although readers are given voice for their opinions, they are confined to one section, of one page, of the paper—the letters to the editor section. Letter writers often go underground by writing anonymously, because in today's climate one can be reprimanded, even fired, for holding to the traditional view of marriage.

Other Media

Attorney and author Michael Snyder writes that in 2010, just six major corporations controlled our media. He named the six as: Time Warner, Walt Disney, Viacom, News Corp., CBS Corporation and NBC Universal. In the article, he said they "own television networks, cable channels, movie studios, newspapers, magazines, publishing houses, music labels and even many of our favorite websites."[1] And by doing so, they "control most of what we watch, hear and read every single day."[2]

So how do these major media corporations stand on the gay "marriage" issue? On the Human Rights Campaign Corporate Equality Index (discussed in Chapter V), Time Warner and Walt Disney scored 100; Viacom and CBS scored 90. NBC and News Corp. were not rated.

And how about the new media, the internet? Yahoo, Google and Microsoft all have news that they offer to the public. How do they score on the Corporate Equality Index? All three have a perfect 100.

Facebook and Twitter are internet social network services. If you have an account with either of these, you might have seen many people change their profile picture (in Twitter it's called an avatar) to the symbol below.

HRC Logo

Cooked?

This symbol is the logo of the Human Rights Campaign. It has a deep blue background with a bright yellow equal sign. Many people used a spin-off of it (a pink equal sign on a red background to symbolize love) for their profile picture or avatar. They were showing their support for gay "marriage" during the time the US Supreme Court was hearing two cases that would affect that issue. The symbol went viral,[3] and an HRC spokesman said he was excited that "public support for marriage equality [is] so great."[4]

Part V

WHY TAKE A STAND FOR NATURAL MARRIAGE?

Now is our chance to choose the right side. . . . [That chance] won't last forever. We must take it or leave it.

~C. S. Lewis

11

GAY "MARRIAGE" NEGATIVELY IMPACTS A CULTURE

The AIDS Epidemic

The AIDS epidemic in America began over 30 years ago, about 1980. The United States Center for Disease Control (CDC) posted on its website that in 2007, MSM (men having sex with men) were forty-four to eighty-six times as likely to be diagnosed with HIV compared with other men.[1] The website stated, "MSM account for just two percent of the US population, but accounted for sixty-one percent of all new HIV infections in 2009."[2] The CDC says there are about 50,000 newly infected people each year.[3]

Referring to the rate of AIDS among homosexuals, even gay activist Matt Foreman admitted:

> Internally, when these numbers come out, the "established" gay community seems to have a collective shrug as if this isn't our problem. Folks, with 70 percent of the people in this country living with HIV being gay or bi[sexual], we cannot deny that HIV is a gay disease. We have to own that and face up to that.[4]

When gay "marriage" is legalized, homosexual behavior is legitimized. Are we, as a culture, willing to tell young men with same-sex attractions to embrace the homosexual lifestyle, even if statistics show their very lives are endangered by doing so?

Group Marriage (Polyamory)

The most common definition of polygamy is a husband having two or more wives. Polyamory includes polygamy, but also a whole lot more. It is defined as: the state or practice of having more than one open romantic relationship at a time.

An example of a polyamorous relationship is the Netherlands cohabitation contract entered into on September 23, 2005. 46-year-old Victor de Bruijn and Bianca, his 31-year-old wife, had been married eight years. They appeared before a notary public in Roosendaal, a small Dutch town. The couple was formally united with Mirjam Geven, a recently divorced 35-year-old woman. The husband Victor claims he is solely heterosexual, but both the women have been having bisexual tendencies, so they are involved romantically as well. These two women and one man are now, under Dutch law, committed in a cohabitation contract.[5]

Some people, especially gay activists, say that gay "marriage" will never, never, never lead to group "marriage." Homosexuals claim that they just want to enjoy the same rights as heterosexuals. However, if they are allowed to "marry" the person they choose, then why should bisexuals be denied "marriage" to the people they choose?

It took the Netherlands from April 1, 2001 (the date gay "marriage" was approved) until September, 2005, just over four years, for the first polyamorists to obtain legal recognition of their "marriage."[6]

Some would say that a cohabitation contract is not the same as a marriage. However, cohabitation contracts were the very vehicle used by Dutch homosexuals in the 1980s to eventually gain "marriage" recognition in 2001.

LGB and T and the Sky's the Limit

Gay activist John Avarosis wrote the article, "How did the T get in LGBT?" He chronicles a little of how the movement picked up steam. It started out as gay, expanded to include lesbian, then "by the early 1990s we were the lesbian, gay and bisexual, or LGB community. Sometime in the late '90s, a few gay rights groups and activists started using a new acronym, LGBT—adding T for transgender/transsexual."[7]

In the article, Mr. Avarosis says that the T hurt their cause. He said the national Employment Non-Discrimination Act (ENDA)[8] was about to pass, but transgender had been added to the bill, and then no one wanted to vote for it. Many gay people, however, felt that they couldn't turn their backs on another persecuted group. Hadn't they themselves felt that same persecution?

What other groups does the LGBT community embrace? BDSM. One definition of BDSM is that it contracts the initials of the following Bondage/Discipline (BD), Dominance/Submission (DS), Sadism/Masochism (SM). Sometimes BDSM might be called "leather." BDSM has not yet been added to the LGBT acronym, but they are embraced by the LGBT community.

They often march in gay pride parades, and on a blogger's "about the author" page, he says of himself:

> Author and columnist Steve Lenius came out as a gay man in 1974 and became involved in the Twin Cities leather community in 1993. For fifteen years his Leather Life column has appeared in *Lavender,* Minnesota's GLBT magazine.[9]

Many homosexuals do just want to have "normal" families (except for having a same-sex "spouse"). However, if we are going to embrace the atypical behavior of homosexuality, we will likely usher in the complete liberation from any sexual mores in our culture.

Test Case: Massachusetts

The following is a summary of Brian Camenker's pamphlet "What same-sex 'marriage' has done to Massachusetts:"[10]

> In November, 2003, the Supreme Court of Massachusetts ruled that it was unconstitutional to deny marriage rights to same-sex couples. Six months later, homosexual "weddings" started to take place.
>
> **How has this affected:**
>
> **Public Schools?** In December of 2003, a Massachusetts high school had a school wide assembly to celebrate same-sex "marriage." By September of 2004, a middle school teacher claimed that the Supreme Court ruling "opened the door for teaching homosexuality" and she was doing that in her eighth-grade classroom. By 2005, elementary students in Lexington, Massachusetts, were given cop-

ies of a picture book that showed same-sex "couples" as an alternate family structure. A father refused to leave a school meeting unless officials would notify him in advance about this kind of school instruction. He was arrested and jailed overnight. In 2006, a teacher read to a second-grade class the book *King and King*, a gay "marriage" story. When parents of one of those students raised objections, they were told the school had no obligation to notify them so they could opt their child out. In 2007, a federal judge ruled, and an appeals court upheld, that because gay "marriage" is legal in Massachusetts, parents have no right to "interfere" when the schools teach about homosexuality. The appeals court ruled that homosexuality and gay "marriage" no longer come under "human sexuality issues" in the Massachusetts parental notification law.

"Gay days" are celebrated in the schools. Even cross-dressing and transsexuality are promoted.

Public Health? Five months after same-sex "marriages" began, a bill signed by Governor Mitt Romney eliminated the need for STD testing, even though there was an increase in syphilis and other STDs in homosexual men in Massachusetts.

The Massachusetts Department of Public Health helped the AIDS Action Committee produce "The Little Black Book: Queer in the 21st Century." The booklet, which explained how to have gay sex and included a directory of gay bars, was handed out to teenagers at Brookline High School in 2005.

Hospitals? Hospitals are "promoting" the gay lifestyle by marching in gay pride parades, holding homosexual events, and putting on several "gay health"-related seminars.

When a doctor objected and stated that he and many others at the hospital where he worked considered homosexual acts unnatural and immoral, the hospital threatened to fire him. After a hearing, he kept his job but was told to keep his opinions to himself.

Business and Employment? All insurance companies must cover, and all businesses must offer benefits to, homosexual "couples." Any employee can be fired for voicing a moral objection to homosexuality.

All wedding industry providers must accommodate same-sex "couples," or be held liable for discrimination.

Public displays of homosexual affection are flaunted in businesses to test their tolerance. If businesses object, they can be fined or punished.

Adoption and Birth Certificates? The state's foster and adoption care workers went through extensive "LGBT youth awareness" training. The sessions were conducted by the National Gay and Lesbian Task Force. The idea promoted was that those working with children must be trained that homosexuality and transgenderism are normal.

Homosexual "couples" must be allowed to adopt children. It seems that adoption agencies are even favoring homosexual "couples."

The Massachusetts Department of Social Services, against the wishes of the birth parents, placed a baby with two men in a same-sex relationship. The Massachusetts Adoption Resource Exchange places large ads in LGBT publications.

Birth certificates don't say "mother" and "father;" they say "mother/parent" and "father/parent." Two men or two women can be on the birth certificate. Homosexuals that adopt can revise children's existing birth certificates. (The other biological parent is not even on the birth certificate.)

Government Mandates? Marriage licenses read "Party A" and "Party B" instead of "husband" and "wife."

In 2004, Governor Mitt Romney ordered all Justices of the Peace to perform homosexual marriages or be fired. Many justices resigned.

In 2008, Massachusetts changed its Medicare laws to include same-sex "couples."

The Public Square? Gay Pride events are more prominent across the state, with more politicians and corporations participating.

Churches? Churches that host pro-marriage or ex-gay seminars, or even present a natural marriage message, have been the target of homosexual protesters. Even though these protesters infringe on people's right to freedom of speech, and often cause people to feel physically threatened, police refuse to take action.

Media? The Boston media often portrays homosexual "couples" where regular married couples would normally be used. Advice columns often deal with issues concerning, or how to properly accept, homosexual "marriage."

Politics? Politicians who support natural marriage keep it to themselves, because they will be accused of wanting to "take away people's rights." Any public discussion on the issue is stifled. Pro-family people across the state are intimidated into silence.

Massachusetts GOP House and Senate leaders both publicly support gay "marriage," along with the recent GOP candidates for governor and lieutenant governor. GOP candidates for office are told not even to discuss it. The new GOP chairman steers clear of the issue. Every state-wide elected official and member of Congress publicly supports gay "marriage."

The Gay "Marriage" Ruling

Gay "marriage" was imposed on Massachusetts by the court, and the governor went along with the decision. The legislature blocked two attempts by the people to amend the state constitution to protect marriage.

Massachusetts still has no law that allows gay "marriage," only a court opinion.

Conclusion

When same-sex "marriage" is legalized, it affects every area of society. The state becomes more powerful, and the people enjoy less freedom.

Homosexual activists, by and large, do not have gay "marriage" as their goal. Though some desire the "right" to marry, most want their lifestyle approved by the culture. They are reaching their goal much faster than any of us would have expected.

(end of summary of "What same-sex 'marriage' has done to Massachusetts")

Consider Some Questions

The teen years are often a time of rebellion. Teenagers push the limits on many things their parents and society forbid. In the past, some things were kept at arm's length, one of them being homosexuality. Question: *As our culture puts its stamp of approval on this behavior, does it not make sense that teenagers will be more likely to experiment with homo-*

sexual acts even if they are not plagued with same-sex attractions?

Someone told this story:

> A middle-aged man, who had same sex-attractions as long as he could remember, was visiting with his young niece. She had married young and had two children. She left her husband to venture off into a romantic relationship with a girlfriend of hers. The middle-aged man was angry with his niece. He had these unwanted same-sex attractions all his life and would never wish them on anyone, but here his niece was choosing to engage in same-sex behavior as something new and vogue. Question: *If we tell young people that homosexual relationships are normal, won't many more young people choose them?*

A study was done to show that children raised in homes of homosexual "couples" were more likely to be homosexual themselves. The gay activists were quick to discredit the study, because it would add credibility to the argument that circumstances contribute to a person's orientation. Question: *Since same-sex "parents" approve of homosexual acts, don't you think that homosexuality will become more prevalent?*

12

THE CASE FOR NATURAL MARRIAGE

What Is the Essential Public Purpose of Marriage?

Part One of the speech, "Same Sex Marriage: Why Not?"[1] by Dr. Jennifer Roeback Morris (All of the following information was taken from the speech. It was changed just in what was needed to make it a written document.)

The purpose for marriage is to attach parents to their children and to each other. There are two reasons the state has an interest in the institution of marriage:

- Human children have a long period of dependency and need to be cared for (preferably by their biological mother and father).

- Humans reproduce sexually, incurring shared responsibility for the offspring thus created.

Private purposes for marriage might be: we want to show we love each other, or we want social approval for our relationship, etc. However, the public purpose for marriage is this: instability of the natural family hurts society.

There is also a public purpose for marriage from the child's point of view: every child has an interest in the stability of their parents' marriage, so they can have a relationship with each of their parents. Children can't defend this interest in court, so we need marriage to proactively protect the legitimate interests of the children.

In order to defend same-sex "marriage," judges need to redefine the purpose of marriage. Judge Vaughn Walker in overturning Proposition 8 [2] defined marriage as the state recognition and approval of a couple's choice to:

- Remain committed to one another

- Form a household based on their own feelings about one another

- Join in an economic partnership to support one

another and any dependents

In this definition he includes nothing about children, and nothing about sex. He disregards the very public purpose for marriage.

How Does Same-sex "Marriage" Hurt Society?

Part Two of Dr. Jennifer Roeback Morris' speech, "Same Sex Marriage: Why Not?"[3]

Natural marriage is something the state has always recognized. It brings stability to families. This is seen in the following four principles:

1. Children ordinarily are entitled to a relationship with their mothers and fathers.

Unwed mothering has started to unravel this principle, because many children are being raised without their fathers. Same-sex "marriage" will further unravel this principle, because children raised in same-sex homes will be denied either a mother or a father.

When a mother gives birth, that child is for sure the offspring of the mother. The father tie is not so obvious. Presumption of paternity is as follows: The husband is presumed to be the father, and ninety-five percent of the time, this is the case.

In approving same-sex "marriage," our society is considering replacing presumption of paternity with presumption of parentage; that means whoever takes on the duties of parenting is the parent. This deliberately excludes one parent of the child.

Marriage usually ties parents to children. Same-sex "marriage" necessarily denies the child one biological parent.

2. Mothers and fathers are not interchangeable. Moms and dads are different. Children need both a mother and a father.

An Iowa judge (in the Iowa Supreme Court ruling that made same-sex "marriage" legal in Iowa) in effect, said, "It's a myth that children need a mother and a father." It's really not a myth. Mothers and fathers make different contributions to their children. Father absence has a different effect than mother absence does. Father absence affects sons more.

Fatherhood has lost its place of prominence. Here are some examples:

- In the United States, we have about a forty percent out-of-wedlock birth rate.

- In the UK, before unmarried women adopted, they had a clause that said there must be a father figure in the child's life. When same-sex "marriage" passed, that requirement was removed.

- In British Columbia (Canada), the birth certificate has a place for the mother's name, but simply a check-off box for the father.

Fatherhood will be further marginalized if same-sex "marriage" is legalized. Fathers will become even less necessary.

3. We define parenthood by biology—motherhood and fatherhood.

Adoption is an exception. Adoption exists to give children the parents they need, not to give parents the children they want.

For an adoption to take place, the biological parents must legally surrender their rights. Those rights are undertaken by the adoptive parents. The biological principle is not undermined; children still have a mother and a father.

Redefining marriage will redefine parenthood. Here are some of the consequences:

- Children will not have two parents, they might have three. Where there is a sperm donor for a lesbian couple in a joint agreement, the law is dealing with three names on the birth certificate.

Children might have four parents, e.g., a gay couple and a lesbian couple decide to produce a child. Biology no longer defines parenthood.

- Children's passports will no longer list mother and father; instead parent A and parent B will be used. A biological mother will have no special standing over her lesbian partner; they will both be equal under the law. This could be problematic as maternal instincts flare. Most mothers will admit, it's hard to share the care of their child with another woman, even a close relative, because mothers are very protective of their children.

4. The state recognizes parentage, but it doesn't assign or control parentage.

When same-sex "marriage" is approved, the state will decide who is the parent. There will be no natural parents, only legal parents, because that privilege will be decided by the state.

The government will look into the cases to see if you "wiped enough noses and changed enough diapers to qualify as a parent."

In natural marriage, government recognizes an already existing reality; in same-sex "marriage," you are creating something new. Natural marriage is self sustaining; same-sex "marriage," being a creation of the state, will need the state to sustain it—to tell it what its boundaries are. Thus, same-sex "marriage" will greatly expand the reach of government.

Here are some examples of state intervention, against the consciences of the individuals or organizations involved:

- The Knights of Columbus will be required to rent out their halls for same-sex "marriages."

- Doctors will be forced to artificially inseminate lesbians.

- Catholic charities will be forced to offer adoption to same-sex "couples."

- States will be required to pay spousal benefits to same-sex "couples" if they give them to opposite sex couples.

All of these scenarios have already taken place. As one can see, the scope of the state dramatically increases when same-sex "marriage" becomes law.

(end of speech, "Same Sex Marriage: Why Not?")

13

AMERICA WAKES UP

No Turning Back

In 2009, the New Hampshire legislature passed gay "marriage." The National Organization for Marriage (NOM), an organization working to uphold natural marriage, wanted to prove that gay "marriage" could be overturned. They poured millions of dollars into the state legislative races and won a veto-proof Republican majority in the House; Republicans outnumbered Democrats by three to one.[1] NOM, however, was disappointed with the results. In 2012, the House voted against the repeal 211-116, and killed the bill. It seems no one wants to be accused of "taking away rights." It's better to stop gay "marriage" before it passes.

And for those of you who think civil unions are a reasonable compromise, consider this blog posted on February 10, 2012, by gay activist Jeremy Hooper:

> Focus on the Family's Carrie Gordon Earll thinks she has us all figured out:
>
>> "Civil union laws are the Trojan horse paving the way for same-sex marriage, there's no doubt about it," said Carrie Gordon Earll, CitizenLink's senior director of Issue Analysis. "So far, passage of civil union or expansive domestic partnership laws has ushered in either legislative or court-ordered same-sex marriage in five states.
>>
>> "The same strategy is operating now in New Jersey and Illinois, where civil union laws are not enough," she added. "So when you hear gay activists ask for civil unions, just replace those two words with 'same-sex marriage.' That's the real goal in every case—redefining marriage for everyone."[2]
>
> Were we ever hiding it? In every state that Carrie mentions, we fought hard for full marriage and only accepted the short-

sighted civil unions compromise so that we could protect our families in the interim. Our loudly, proudly stated goal is marriage equality in all fifty states and federally. This is not something we're only talking about in our top secret Gay Agenda meetings—we've made ourselves known.[3]

He's Naked!

Chuck Colson came up with the analogy of how our culture is like the people in the old fairy tale, "The Emperor's New Clothes."

The story goes like this:

The Emperor is a vain man who loves to admire himself in a variety of outfits. Two swindlers convince him that they can make him the most stylish of clothing. They pretend to be weaving invisible clothing on their looms. They claim that only stupid people cannot see their fabric. The emperor brings in two officials and then a group of men. They, and even the emperor himself, claim that they can see the invisible cloth. All the people in the kingdom have been told how the emperor's invisible clothes will be visible to "smart" people. The emperor "dresses" for and then participates in a parade. All the people admire his clothes . . . until a child cries out that the emperor has no clothes on. The people begin considering that this might be true.

This story demonstrates the power of peer pressure. People are willing to go along with the crowd, even if it means denying what they know to be true.

For the past forty years, activists have been telling Americans (and for that matter, people around the globe) that to be gay is OK. Some people think that accepting gays is part of evolving into the modern age.

The child in the fairy tale personifies the hope that one day the majority of the American people will realize that they were right all along—homosexual acts are not natural.

Part **VI**

WHAT CAN WE DO?

*What matters is the sincerity and
perseverance of our will to overcome
[our difficulties].*

~C. S. Lewis

14

ACTION POINTS

Possibilities

Are Americans wanting to take their country back from gay activists? Sometimes, it appears hopeless. I wrote a list of possible action points:

1. Politics:

    - Be wary of negative ads against conservatives, even in the primaries. After an election, one candidate tried to sue for slander, but lost in court because the judge ruled to the effect that politics is a blood sport.

    - Access voter guides to know where candidates

Cooked?

stand on the issues.

- Educate yourself on laws under consideration by state and national legislative bodies. Then let your legislators know what you think about the issues.

2. Schools:

- Run for your local school boards, and know what's going on at your children's school.

- At the beginning of the elementary school year, let your child's teacher know that you don't want your child to participate in any anti-bullying or sex education classes. Let the teacher know that you will conduct that instruction at home. If your school has No Name-Calling Week or Ally Week, ask that your child be opted out.

- At the beginning of the high school year, let the administration know that if any pro-homosexual material is presented, you want equal time spent on presenting the opposing view.

- Keep your children out of school if the school

108

allows students to remain quiet during instruction time on the Day of Silence. It costs schools money when children are absent.

3. Television:

   • Don't allow your children to view programs (or movies) that feature gay and transgender individuals, because they are usually portrayed positively. Don't watch those shows yourself.

4. Corporate America:

   • Contact corporate offices and ask them not to support Gay Pride events.

   • Don't buy products or services from companies that rank high on the Corporate Equality Index of the Human Rights Campaign.

5. National organizations:

   • Consider leaving and/or taking your sons out of Boy Scouts. Onmyhonor.net is working to organize an alternative program that will uphold the Boy Scouts' time-tested standards.

   • Consider dropping your membership in

national organizations that are promoting gay rights, e.g., NEA, APA, NASW.

6. Newspapers:

- Talk to your local newspaper editor and ask him or her to present a balanced approach to covering the topic.

- If your newspaper relies heavily on Associated Press stories and is not a declared conservative voice, know that you may get a one-sided view. Consider canceling your subscription.

Swimming Against the Tide

These possible action points give us a game plan. However, we are swimming into a tidal wave, and there will be opposition in each of these areas just discussed.

1. Politics—If a candidate has access to enough money, it seems he can buy his position.

Gay activists are more involved in the political process than their opponents. When the Boy Scouts were being asked to reconsider their position, gay activists rallied. They secured signatures numbering about twenty-five percent of the gay community. Conservatives were only able to muster signatures of about three tenths of a percent of their numbers.

2. Schools—Many faculty, and some school board members, are the ones supporting these school programs. Even if you get on the school board, your influence could be insignificant.

3. Television—People become attached to programs they enjoy and may not be willing to give them up.

4. Corporate America—One might need to look at buying from companies outside the US, as corporate America appears sold out. These companies are now so committed to "diversity" that it seems like they would be willing to suffer financial loss before they go back on their commitment to LGBT rights.

5. People have come to love the Boy Scout organization, and many are heavily invested in it. It will be very hard for them to leave. Gay rights advocate Ross Murray predicts that less than five percent[1] will leave, that those leaving will make some noise, and then life will go on.

    Ties with other organizations will also be hard to break.

6. Newspapers—Newspapers in large cities general-
    ly support gay rights. Vital Voice, an LGBT news
    source, stated, "Marriage equality legislation has
    been endorsed by nearly every major newspaper
    in Illinois, including: the *Chicago Tribune*, the
    Chicago Sun-Times, the *Daily Herald* [a subur-
    ban Chicago paper], the *Peoria Journal Star*, the
    Springfield Journal-Register, and the *St. Louis
    Post-Dispatch*."[2]

    As early as 1987, a gay activist said, "We have
    captured the liberal establishment and the press.
    We have already beaten you on a number of bat-
    tlefields. And we have the spirit of the age on our
    side. You have neither the faith nor the strength
    to fight us, so you might as well surrender now."[3]

The outlook for America does look bleak, but that doesn't
mean we ought to give up.

Giving to ex-gay ministries and organizations that support natural marriage could prove helpful. Some ex-gay ministries are: Restored Hope Network, Journey into Manhood
(JiM), Homosexuals Anonymous, and Desert Streams/Living
Waters. Most states have family policy councils that work to
support natural marriage, and the National Organization for
Marriage is working toward that end on a national level.

A more comprehensive list of things we might do can be
found at http://aqueerthing.com/content/get-involved.

15

FROM A CHRISTIAN STANDPOINT

Clobber Passages

If "clobber passages" is typed into Google, a person soon learns what the phrase means. Several websites go to great lengths to discredit each clobber passage—each biblical passage that is used to condemn homosexuality. Some websites claim there are six clobber passages, and others claim that there are as many as ten.

The Bible is not just lists of what is right and what is wrong. However, if someone wants to know what the Bible says about different behaviors, she can look up different passages and read them. For example, if she wants to know what the Bible says about stealing, she can use a concordance (a book that alphabetizes and gives the scripture reference for every word in the Bible) and look up the word "steal." She could read what those passages say. Then, since thieves steal, she might look up "thief" or "theft." After looking up the various passages on these words, she can then say she has an idea of how God feels about stealing.

In order to see what God says about homosexuality, you can type "clobber passages" into a search engine and find what the Bible says. Don't read any further on the internet. Just write down those scripture references and look them up in the Bible.

Scripture appears to condemn homosexual behavior, just like God condemns stealing. If you showed someone the scriptures that condemn stealing, you would not be clobbering them with those passages. You would be performing a loving act, because God tells us that thieves will not inherit the kingdom of heaven. It is the same with scripture passages that condemn homosexuality. God doesn't want Christians to clobber people who struggle with same-sex attractions, but he wants the truth to be told in love.

Old Testament Scriptures

Two Old Testament Bible passages speak clearly about homosexuality.

- Lev 18:22 Do not have sexual relations with a man as one does with a woman; that is detestable.

- Lev 20:13a If a man has sexual relations with a man as one does with a woman, both of them have done what is detestable.

Some will argue that if you are going to use Old Testament passages, there are also laws in Leviticus that forbid things like eating shellfish and wearing clothing that mixes fibers. I know of no Christian faith that forbids eating shrimp or wearing clothes made of blended fabric, e.g., polyester and cotton. So is the Old Testament irrelevant for today?

In the Old Testament, God wanted his people set apart from the rest of the people on the face of the earth. He set very strict rules for them to abide by. In the midst of all those rules, he said, "Be holy, because I am holy." God's people were set apart by the sign of circumcision and by their strict adherence to the law. When Jesus came, a new covenant was established. Because of Jesus' death on the cross, all people were invited to be part of God's family. Circumcision and adherence to the law were no longer the way to get right with God. Every person could come to God by turning from their way of living and surrendering themselves to God's will through Jesus Christ.

The early church struggled with this idea. Jews were having a hard time accepting the fact that God would accept non-

Jews who didn't get circumcised, or who didn't strictly follow the law that God had given them. The apostles gathered in Jerusalem to decide the matter. The council made a major decision for all the churches that were starting up. Acts 15:20 says, " . . . we should write to them, telling them to abstain from food polluted by idols, from sexual immorality, from the meat of strangled animals and from blood." Very offensive to the Jewish mind was idolatry, the eating of blood, and sexual immorality.

So that the church could move forward and find unity between the Jews and non-Jews, the apostles settled on a few common restrictions. The new converts need not be circumcised or follow the entire Jewish law, but they were asked to refrain from eating blood—and by extension strangled animals. They were asked not to eat meat that was offered to idols and to stay away from sexual immorality. Where were they to get these guidelines for sexual morality? Leviticus 18 and 20. These chapters forbid a variety of interfamily sexual relations, i.e., incest. They also forbid adultery, homosexuality, and bestiality. One preacher summed it up nicely: For Christians, any sex outside of one man, one woman marriage is unacceptable.

New Testament Scriptures

Three New Testament scripture passages expressly forbid homosexuality: I Cor 6:9-10, Rom 1:26-27, and I Tim 1:9-10. The first passage is from the book of Corinthians:

> I Cor 6:9-10 Or do you not know that wrong-doers will not inherit the kingdom of God? Do not be deceived: Neither the sexually immoral nor idolaters nor adulterers nor men who have sex with men nor thieves nor the greedy nor drunkards nor slanderers nor swindlers will inherit the kingdom of God.

This is taken from the New International Version of the Bible. Other Bible versions might use the word "sodomite" or "homosexual" in the place of "men who have sex with other men."

In Romans, chapter 1, Paul says that men are not acknowledging God in their lives. He continues:

> Rom 1:26-27 Because of this, God gave them over to shameful lusts. Even their women exchanged natural sexual relations for unnatural ones. In the same way the men also abandoned natural relations with women and were inflamed with lust for one another. Men committed shameful acts with other men, and received in themselves the due penalty for their error.

Paul shares the third passage in his letter to Timothy.

> I Tim 1:9-10 We also know that the law is

> made not for the righteous but for lawbreak-
> ers and rebels, the ungodly and sinful, the un-
> holy and irreligious, for those who kill their
> fathers or mothers, for murderers, for the
> sexually immoral, for those practicing ho-
> mosexuality, for slave traders and liars and
> perjurers—and for whatever else is contrary
> to the sound doctrine.

Besides these three New Testament scriptures that forbid homosexuality, there are at least twenty more that tell us to stay away from sexual immorality.

Today, Christians are faced with a choice. If they use the scriptures as their standard, they find that God disapproves of homosexual acts. On the other hand, if they listen to today's culture: movies, television, many teachers, newspapers, etc., they will conclude that homosexuality is simply an alternative lifestyle.

Uphold Strict Standards *and* Welcome Sinners

Dr. Robert Gagnon, an associate professor of New Testament at the Pittsburgh Theological Seminary, has been defending the orthodox Christian view since 2001 that participating in homosexual acts is a grave moral offense. He has a blog where he responds to people who support the opposite position.

In replying[1] to one person, he said what might be appropriate to say to churches that embrace homosexuality:

> Jesus welcomed sinners, but he upheld strict standards; he condemned their sin, and told them to "sin no more."
>
> The Pharisees upheld strict standards and did not welcome sinners; they kept sinners out altogether.
>
> You welcome sinners and do not uphold standards; you allow them to continue in sin, and in doing so you endanger the very salvation of their souls.

Our Hope

So, what can Christians do? My belief is that our best hope is prayer. If Christians all across our nation would gather with like-minded believers to pray for our nation for one hour each week, we might see the mighty hand of God move on our behalf. A web address that shows how to start your own prayer meeting is www.pathlightspress.com/start.html.

In I Kings, chapter 19, Elijah wanted to give up; he felt like all of Israel was against him and he alone was fighting for God. God revealed himself to Elijah, and then God told him he had some specific things he wanted him to do. As an added word of encouragement, God told Elijah there were still seven thousand people serving him in Israel. We can be assured that God has specific things for us to do if we seek his face. We

Cooked?

also know there are many Christians living in our land.

A book I read a few years ago made this observation: A church did a survey of the most flourishing of its ministries. At the top of that list were some ministries headed by former homosexuals.

People like me, who have been saved from sinful lives, are very grateful for that salvation. We desire to give back to God for what he has given us. This is true of those saved from homosexual sin; those who have been freed are very grateful. Also, once they leave the lifestyle, they realize the only way they can stay pure is by a daily surrender of their will to God. This is the very attitude God desires of all people.

Therefore, we can specifically pray for those in the homosexual community. Statistics show that in the United States we could have as many as nine million (and rising fast) adults who identify as homosexual. If God sent heavy conviction resulting in the salvation of a number of that people group, imagine what could happen.

AFTERWORD

Gay rights have been advancing at lightning speed. In just two month's time—from May to June, 2013:

- Three states passed gay "marriage" in their legislative bodies.
- The Boy Scouts of America board voted to allow openly gay scouts.
- Exodus International, the world's largest ex-gay ministry, closed its doors.
- The Supreme Court ruled that gay "couples" who are federal employees are eligible for marriage benefits.
- Gay "marriage" was reinstated in California.

It might appear we are losing the war. However, there is still reason for hope. The battle in Illinois was not lost. Big political players including President Obama, former President Clinton, both of Illinois' national senators, Kirk and Durbin, and Chicago's mayor, Rahm Emanuel, were pushing for the passage of gay "marriage." It passed in the Illinois Senate, and the governor promised to sign it into law. Less than a dozen courageous state representatives stood their ground and refused to commit to voting for a bill that did not reflect the will of their constituents. Gay "marriage" did not pass.

The abortion battle gives us another reason for hope. In 1973, the Supreme Court overruled the will of thirty-three states where abortion was forbidden; it made abortion legal in all fifty states. Pro-choice advocates predicted that the trend would continue and America would one day be one hundred percent pro-choice. Pro-life advocates have been striving for forty years to educate the public about the truth of abortion. Now, a majority of people in our country believe abortions are morally wrong.

Even if our courts, our legislatures, or the vote of the people impose gay "marriage" on our country (or individual states) we shouldn't think that it's going to one day be universally accepted. If good people stand up for what's right—if they care about our country and its future generations—public opinion will eventually take the side of truth. America has made many mistakes, but eventually she gets it right.

RECOMMENDED READING/VIEWING

A Queer Thing Happened in America: And What a Long, Strange Trip It's Been, by Michael L. Brown (available on Kindle). I highly recommend Mr. Brown's book. It was written with the same intent as this book—to inform the American public. Whereas *Cooked?* is a quick read for the average person, *A Queer Thing* is very lengthy, and geared toward those who desire more information.

Homosexuality and the Politics of Truth, by Jeffrey Satinover. Mr. Satinover is an M.D. He gives a medical perspective and writes with great sensitivity.

A Strong Delusion: Confronting the "Gay Christian" Movement, by Joe Dallas. Mr. Dallas was once a member of a "gay Christian" church, but he always had a nagging sense that his lifestyle was not right. Since he left the lifestyle, he has written this and other good books on the topic of homosexuality.

Cooked?

Beyond the Shades of Gray: Because Homosexuality is a Symptom, not a Solution, by Dean Bailey. Mr. Bailey once struggled with homosexuality as well. He speaks as a man mostly to other men. Since he now lives as a Christian family man, he uses much scripture in the book. I disagree with some of what he considers appropriate manly affection on page 167, but overall the content is excellent.

"What same-sex 'marriage' has done to Massachusetts," by Brian Camenker. This is an online document that can be found at: http://www.massresistance.org/docs/marriage/effects_of_ssm_2012/index.html. It was summarized in Chapter VI.

"Homosexual Orientation and the 'Ten Percent' Myth," by the American Life League. This article can be found at: http://ewtn.com/library/prolenc/encyc116.htm. The article covers the American Psychiatric Association's decision covered in Chapter V.

Robert Gagnon's website is http://robgagnon.net. He has written extensively on the subject of homosexuality from a theological point of view.

"Same Sex Marriage: Why Not?" is a speech given by Dr. Jennifer Roeback Morse. This video can be viewed at: http://www.youtube.com/watch?v=I7AwGxqjPWg. It was summarized in Chapter VII.

NOTES

All C. S. Lewis quotes are taken from his book *Mere Christianity*.

Chapter 1

1 Greytak E.A., Kosciw, J.G. & Jerman, K. (2008). No Name-Calling Week Project: Year Four Evaluation. New York: GLSEN. http://www.nonamecallingweek.org/binary-data/NoNameCalling_AT-TACHMENTS/file/151-1, accessed May 17, 2013.
2 The Day of Silence was actually started at the University of Virginia in 1996, but its organization and funding was taken over by GLSEN in 2001.
3 http://www.nonamecallingweek.org/cgi-bin/iowa/all/about/index.html, accessed May 17, 2013.
4 Ibid.
5 http://www.allyweek.org/about/, accessed May 17, 2013.
6 http://sports.glsen.org/, accessed May 17, 2013.
7 http://sports.glsen.org/a-physical-education-climate-check-list/, accessed June 4, 2013
8 https://www.revisor.mn.gov/statutes/?id=121a.0695, accessed May 17, 2013.
9 http://www.startribune.com/politics/statelocal/194096251.html?refer=y, accessed May 17, 2013.
10 http://www.twincities.com/education/ci_22693440/at-capitol-legislature-takes-up-anti-bullying-proposal, accessed May 17, 2013.

Chapter 2

1. http://www.glsen.org/cgi-bin/iowa/all/library/record/2342.html, accessed May 17, 2013.
2. http://www.gsanetwork.org/about-us/faq, accessed May 17, 2013.
3. http://www.ontla.on.ca/web/bills/bills_detail.do?locale=en&BillID=2549, accessed May 17, 2013.
4. http://www.gale.cengage.com/greenhaven/greenhaven.htm, accessed May 17, 2013.
5. http://community.pflag.org/page.aspx?pid=191, accessed May 17, 2013.
6. Ibid.
7. http://www.webfieldtrips.com/PSY210doc/WhosGay.pdf, accessed May 17, 2013.
8. http://pfox.org/ex-gay-questions-answers.pdf, accessed May 17, 2013.

Chapter 3

1. http://www.yale.edu/oldYaleInfo/studentorgs.html, accessed May 17, 2013.
2. http://wc.asu.edu/pages/diversity-groups-and-resources/what-types-lgbt-groupsorganizations-are-available-students-asu, accessed May 17, 2013.
3. http://www.youtube.com/watch?v=YvIEq3kWPYQ&feature=player_embedded, accessed May 17, 2013.
4. http://illinoisfamily.org/education/gustavus-adolphus-college-promotes-perversion-to-freshmen/, accessed May 17, 2013.
5. http://www.soulforce.org/about/, accessed May 18, 2013.
6. http://www.gayalliance.org/safezonet.html, accessed May 17, 2013.
7. http://www.unlv.edu/event/training-campus-wide-safe-zone?delta=2, accessed May 9, 2013.
8. http://www.rhodes.edu/campuslife/11503.asp, accessed May 9, 2013.

Chapter 4

1 http://goaskalice.columbia.edu/how-do-i-know-if-im-gay, accessed May 17, 2013.
2 http://gaylife.about.com/od/howtocomeout/a/How-To-Tell-If-You-Are-Really-Gay.htm, accessed May 17, 2013.
3 http://www.phatpage.org/howdoiknow.html, accessed May 18, 2013.
4 http://www.itgetsbetter.org/pages/about-it-gets-better-project/, accessed May 18, 2013.
5 Quoted in *Homosexuality and the Politics of Truth* by Jeffrey Satinover, M.D., Hamewith Books, 1996, pp. 266-267. Original quote from Gary Remafedi, James A. Farrow, Robert W. Deisher. "Risk Factors for Attempted Suicide in Gay and Bisexual Youth," *Pediatrics* 87, no. 6 (1991), pp. 869-75.

Chapter 5

1 http://www.livestrong.com/article/222032-how-much-tv-does-the-average-child-watch-each-day/, accessed May 17, 2013.
2 http://www.tv.com/news/glaad-gay-tv-characters-declining-10215/, accessed May 17, 2013.
3 http://www.glaad.org/publications/whereweareontv12, accessed May 17, 2013.
4 http://blog.nielsen.com/nielsenwire/media_entertainment/the-new-mainstream-28-of-tv-watching-spent-on-lgbt-inclusive-shows/, accessed May 17, 2013.
5 http://popwatch.ew.com/2011/01/21/gay-teens-do-they-belong-on-the-tween-networks/, accessed May 17, 2013.

Chapter 6

1 http://www.lyricsmode.com/lyrics/k/katy_perry/i_kissed_a_girl.html, accessed May 17, 2013.
2 http://www.lyrics.com/same-love-lyrics-macklemore.html, accessed May 17, 2013.
3 http://www.nytimes.com/2010/11/07/fashion/07ANTHEM.html?pagewanted=2&_r=0, accessed May 17, 2013.

Chapter 7

1   http://www.hrc.org/resources/entry/stances-of-faiths-on-lgbt-issues-metropolitan-community-churches, accessed May 18, 2013.

2   http://www.religiousinstitute.org/religious-declaration-on-sexual-morality-justice-and-healing, accessed May 17, 2013.

3   http://www.religiousinstitute.org/healthyseminaries, accessed May 18, 2013.

Chapter 8

1   http://www.nomblog.com/category/marriage-election-watch?doing_wp_cron, Brian Brown, *Election Results Should "Wake Up and Energize" Marriage Advocates,* Nov, 2012, accessed May 18, 2013.

2   http://leginfo.legislature.ca.gov/faces/billNavClient.xhtml?bill_id=201120120SB1172, accessed May 18, 2013.

3   http://www.njleg.state.nj.us/2012/Bills/S2500/2278_I1.PDF, accessed May 18, 2013.

4   http://www.hrc.org/files/assets/resources/Housing_Laws_and_Policies (1).pdf, accessed May 18, 2013.

5   http://www.hrc.org/files/assets/resources/Employment_Laws_and_Policies.pdf, accessed May 18, 2013.

6   http://www.stopbullying.gov/laws/index.html, accessed May 18, 2013.

7   http://www.ncsl.org/issues-research/human-services/same-sex-marriage-overview.aspx, accessed May 18, 2013.

8   Ibid.

9   http://www.hrc.org/marriage-center, accessed May 18, 2013.

10 http://www.hrc.org/files/assets/resources/joint_adoption_parenting_laws_dec2012.pdf, accessed May 18, 2013.

11 http://www.hrc.org/files/assets/resources/hate_crime_laws.pdf, accessed May 18, 2013.

12 Ibid.

13 http://www.democrats.org/democratic-national-platform#protecting-rights, accessed May 17, 2013.

14 http://www.gop.com/2012-republican-platform_Renewing/, accessed May 17, 2013.

15 Most of the info in this article is taken from *They Won't Know What Hit Them* by Joshua Green, Atlantic, March, 2007, at http://www.theatlantic.com/magazine/archive/2007/03/they-won-t-know-what-hit-them/305619/5/, accessed May 18, 2013.

16 http://gillfoundation.org/media/about-us/, accessed May 18, 2013.

17 http://www.nydailynews.com/news/politics/cost-u-s-senate-seat-10-5-million-article-1.1285491, accessed May 18, 2013.

18 http://www.dailykos.com/story/2012/05/07/1089543/-Super-PACs-12-million-already-poured-into-state-level-races, accessed May 18, 2013.

Chapter 9

1 ewtn.com/library/prolenc/encyc116.htm, , accessed May 18, 2013.

2 Satinover, Jeffrey, M.D., *Homosexuality and the Politics of Truth*, Baker Books, 1996, p. 35

3 A lengthier explanation can be read at ewtn.com/library/prolenc/encyc116.htm in the section entitled *THE AMERICAN PSYCHIATRIC ASSOCIATION COUP.*

4 Don't Ask, Don't Tell was the military's policy that allowed gay members to serve, but to keep that fact that they were homosexual private.

5 http://www.apa.org/about/policy/military.aspx, accessed May 18, 2013.

6 Ibid.

7 http://www.nea.org/home/55038.htm, accessed May 18, 2013.

8 Ibid.

9 http://pediatrics.aappublications.org/content/131/4/e1374.full#abstract-1, accessed May 24, 2013.

10 http://www.ama-assn.org/ama/pub/about-ama/our-people/member-groups-sections/glbt-advisory-committee/ama-policy-regarding-sexual-orientation.page, accessed May 24, 2013.

11 http://www.socialworkers.org/advocacy/letters/2012/Testimony for the Senate Committee on Health Education Labor and Pensions RE Employment Non-Discrimination Act.pdf, accessed May 24, 2013.

12 http://www.socialworkers.org/pubs/news/2010/06/default.asp, accessed May 18, 2013.

13 http://www.hrc.org/the-hrc-story/about-us, accessed May 18, 2013.

14 The 2013 CEI can be viewed at http://www.hrc.org/files/assets/resources/CEI_2013_Final_low.pdf.pdf or http://issuu.com/humanrightscampaign/docs/corporateequalityindex_2013

15 http://www.hrc.org/files/assets/resources/CEI_2013_Final_low.pdf.pdf, p 14, accessed June 1, 2013.

16 http://www.onmyhonor.net/impact-of-open-homosexuality-in-scouting/, accessed June 1, 2013.

17 http://www.reuters.com/article/2013/05/23/us-usa-boyscouts-ban-vote-idUSBRE94M1A320130523, accessed May 23, 2013.

18 http://www.christianpost.com/news/boy-scouts-were-pressured-by-corporate-sponsors-to-change-policy-on-gays-89156/, accessed June 2, 2013

19 Ibid.

20 http://www.scouting.org/filestore/about/AnnualReports/pdf/2012_TreasurerReport.pdf, accessed June 2, 2013.

21 http://www.reuters.com/article/2013/05/23/us-usa-boyscouts-ban-vote-idUSBRE94M1A320130523, accessed May 23, 2013.

Chapter 10

1 http://theeconomiccollapseblog.com/archives/who-owns-the-media-the-6-monolithic-corporations-that-control-almost-everything-we-watch-hear-and-read, accessed May 15, 2013.

2 Ibid.

3 The Urban Dictionary says "go viral" is used in reference to Internet content which can be passed through electronic mail and social networking sites (Facebook, etc.): an image, video, or link that spreads rapidly through a population by being frequently shared with a number of individuals has "gone viral."

4 http://tv.msnbc.com/2013/03/26/seeing-red-human-rights-campaigns-marriage-equality-logo-goes-viral/, accessed May 18, 2013.

Chapter 11

1 http://www.cdc.gov/hiv/topics/msm/index.htm, accessed April 2, 2012. Note: Both this address and footnote #2 redirect to a new and updated page. I copied the pages from which I took this information in April, 2012. I can no longer find this information on the CDC site.

2 http://www.cdc.gov/hiv/resources/factsheets/us.htm, accessed April 2, 2012. See note on footnote #1, above.

3 http://www.cdc.gov/hiv/basics/statistics.html, accessed May 18, 2013.

4 http://www.lifesitenews.com/news/archive/ldn/2010/mar/10031715, accessed May 18, 2013.

5 This story is taken from *Here Come the* Brides by Stanley Kurtz, The Weekly Standard, Dec, 2005 at http://www.weeklystandard.com/Content/Public/Articles/000/000/006/494pqobc.asp?page=1, accessed May 18, 2013.

6 Ibid.

7 http://www.salon.com/2007/10/08/lgbt/, accessed May 9, 2013.

8 See Part I for an explanation of ENDA.

9 http://www.lifeleatherpursuit.com/author, accessed May 18, 2013.

10 http://www.massresistance.org/docs/marriage/effects_of_ssm.html, accessed May 18, 2013.

Chapter 12

1 The entire speech can be viewed at http://www.youtube.com/watch?v=I7AwGxqjPWg.

2 Prop 8 is explained in Part I, The Basics: Definitions. Judge Walker overturned that decision when it was taken to court.

3 The entire speech can be viewed at http://www.youtube.com/watch?v=I7AwGxqjPWg.

Chapter 13

1 http://www.nytimes.com/2012/03/22/us/politics/new-hampshire-refuses-to-repeal-gay-marriage-right.html?_r=0, accessed May 18, 2013.

2   http://www.citizenlink.com/2012/02/09/washington-house-pass-
    es-same-sex-marriage-bill/, accessed May 18, 2013.
3   http://www.goodasyou.org/good_as_you/2012/02/civil-unions-
    are-a-trojan-horse-nay.html, accessed May 18, 2013.

Chapter 14
1   http://abcnews.go.com/US/churches-sever-ties-boy-scouts-lifted-
    ban-gay/story?id=19270860&page=2#.Uar1LpyjIyg, accessed
    June 1, 2013.
2   http://www.thevitalvoice.com/news/50-latest-news/845-mar-
    riage-equality-momentum-brings-together-new-illinois-coalition,
    accessed May 27, 2013.
3   http://www.afajournal.org/2006/february/206GayWar.asp, ac-
    cessed May 18, 2013.

Chapter 15
1   http://robgagnon.net/articles/homosexmarinloveisorientation.
    pdf, accessed May 18, 2013.

INDEX

Cooked?